Babysitters!

AND OTHER ADVICE

FOR RAISING A CHILD

Babysitters!

AND OTHER ADVICE FOR

RAISING A CHILD

MARLOE PRESS

NEW YORK

MARLOE PRESS
Copyright © 2015

Printed and bound in the U.S.A.

ISBN 978-0-9823495-2-6

*Designed and composed by
Jenny Carrow and Abby Kagan
based upon the design by Gretchen Achilles*

Block illustration by Sara Mills

www.marloepress.com

Babysitters!

Have patience.

Be encouraging.

Respect their fears.

Go easy on the sugar.

Read together.

Laugh together.

Let them know you're proud of them.

*Take pictures—
but not constantly.*

Be forgiving.

Don't talk down to them.

Love them without conditions.

Have rules.

Break the rules.

Answer questions honestly.

From time to time, go out without them.

Learn together.

Let them fail.

Be the example.

Kiss them when they're sleeping.

Play chase.

Be consistent.

Have rewards and consequences.

Listen.

Be firm.

Let them know they matter.

Travel.

Celebrate.

Ask questions.

Teach them to say please and thank you.

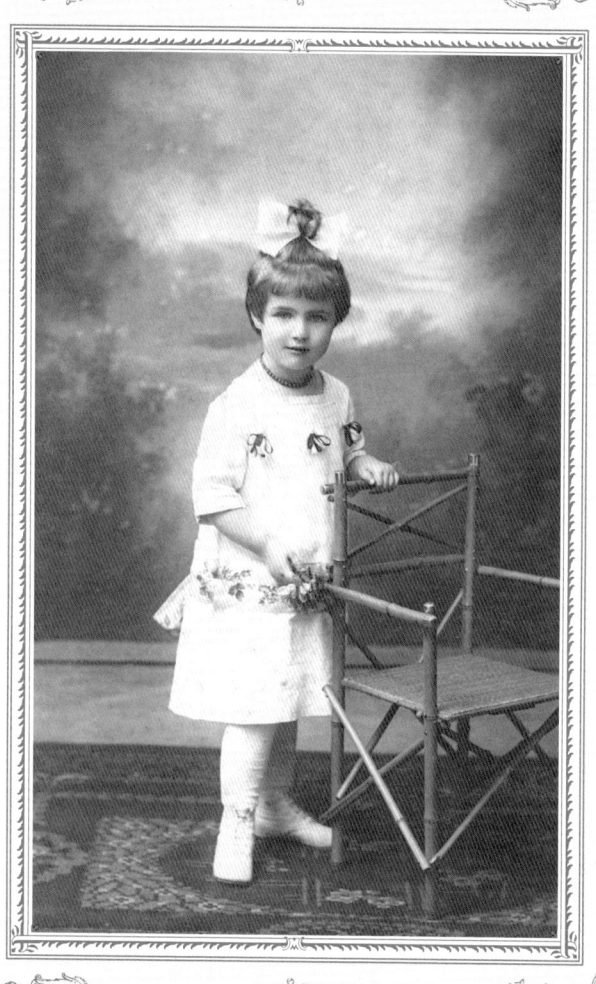

Let them win, but also let them lose.

Make art.

Don't yell.

Show them what family means.

Try to imagine life without them.

Additional Advice